T0114559

A FEW GOOD MEN

A PATH TO GODLY FATHERHOOD

Brother Prater

authorHOUSE®

AuthorHouse™
1663 Liberty Drive
Bloomington, IN 47403
www.authorhouse.com
Phone: 1 (800) 839-8640

Published by AuthorHouse 02/15/2016

ISBN: 978-1-5049-5529-4 (sc)
ISBN: 978-1-5049-5528-7 (e)

Library of Congress Control Number: 2016902395

Credits: Copy Editor by KG Edits

Photos by: Logan's Photography
Perfect Images Photography
Olan Mills

Scripture quotations marked KJV are from the Holy Bible, King James Version (Authorized Version). First published in 1611. Quoted from the KJV Classic Reference Bible, Copyright © 1983 by The Zondervan Corporation.

Print information available on the last page.

Forwards by:
Derrick Richardson
and
Deborah Freeman

My reason and desire to be a part of this particular book is genuinely of gratitude. I am deeply and truly thankful for the friendship of not just the man, but the minister of Brother Prater. I have known him for over twenty years. I have witnessed a powerful and phenomenal God ordained shift in his ministry in the past seven years. I have watched his gifting manifest and grow from discernment, word of knowledge, word of wisdom, and into his now powerfully manifested gift of teaching.

I believe it is evident of his God-given teaching gift that it has led him to the current writing of this much needed book. Spiritual written books are usually birth through personal experience and God-ordained process. It is a process in which we as ministers are crushed as in a biblical winepress. This produces much needed anointed and Godly ripe fruit.

I have witnessed some of the process in Brother Prater's experience in this particular subject matter. He has embodied the teaching of the father in a totally God-inspired view. It is not strange or awkward that God would choose such a man as Brother Prater to minister on such a highly priority message of this caliber.

The secular world as well as some professing Christian men are in great dearth of being true Godly fathers. I have been blessed to read this book and obtain much needed biblical views to fulfilling my role as a Godly father. I was enlightened by new revelations as well as reignited in dormant areas as a father.

I would also encourage mothers of every ethnic group to read this very informative book, as Brother Prater has included wise and knowledgeable nuggets for them as well. I thank God for the anointed vessel of Brother Prater and his availability and willingness to the plan of God in the earth realm. My prayer is that this book reaches the masses to whom it is ordained and manifest much Godly righteous fruit!!! We truly and undeniably now need "A FEW GOOD MEN"!!

Derrick Richardson

Brother Prater,

I've met a lot of people, but no one quite like you. I knew from the start that there was something special about you. You were unassuming and soft spoken. Me being your training officer, I use to tell you to speak up because you sounded like a cat meowing. I still smile when I think about the expression on your face.

That was 20 years ago and look at you now! You're a force to be reckon with! You have made positive impacts in the lives of many. Your audience listens to you and your words of wisdom. I personally love to watch your videos! They are directly from God! He has given you discernment and a voice to deliver powerful words of encouragements and hope.

Now as you offer your gifts into this book, it is definitely a must read! It will minister to women as well as men! May God's blessings be upon this book and those who read it!

Deborah Freeman

My daddy and I (1972)

Contents

Santa, My Daddy and I (1973)

Daddy and I

My Personal Acknowledgements

I would like to thank my personal Savior, Jesus Christ for blessing me to give birth to this book. I take it as a great privilege and responsibility. I would like to dedicate this book to my son, Dillon. You are the driving force of why I do what I do! Daddy loves you very much!

To my dad, Charles Prater Sr., you are the strongest, wisest man I have ever known. To my mother, Ruby Prater, the best dresser and cook that has ever walk the earth. If she knows you, she always wants to cook for you! To my brothers (Jerry, Ronnie, and Walter), I appreciate and love you all dearly! To my FAVORITE, SMART and ONLY sister (we're NOT twins - we're 362 days apart), thank you for ALWAYS looking out for your big brother! Love you much!!

To my pastor and his wife (my friends, family, mentors and 2nd parents) Otis and Ollie Logan. To the GREATEST Sunday School teacher / Bible teacher, Landolph (Landy) Washington, thank you so much for your wisdom, love and patience! My god-parents Minister Tim & Sister Mae Green, a host of family, friends and amazing people I have had the honor to meet in my life! You have all played a key role in helping me become the man I am today! Thank You!

Love,
Little June

In memory of my cousin and best friend Kelvin Logan

Me (1975)

Introduction

In my 20+ years in law enforcement, I've seen many results of fatherless children. I've seen children visit their fathers in jail and ask, "Daddy, when are you coming home?" I've witnessed kids crying at the top of their lungs because visiting hours were over and they saw their fathers in handcuffs being escorted back to their jail cells. It becomes a regular routine for me to see a child grow up before my eyes at the jail. There were some occasions when I ended up walking young men into the same jail cell where their fathers use to be.

I have also heard many frustrating stories of how some fathers were prevented from seeing their own children by the children's mother. There have been countless stories of a father receiving injustice with the courts in relation to child support and visitation rights, or the father being punished by the mother or society because of a failed romantic relationship with the children's mother. There are fathers who have been on child support, yet they have not seen their children in weeks, months or even years. When fathers are restricted from seeing or raising their children, it takes a toll on the children, the families, communities and churches.

This book is to celebrate those fathers who are taking care of their responsibilities; to challenge those who are not; to promote women to acknowledge and appreciate a child's father who is fulfilling his role; and to educate single women on the qualities they should look for in their potential husband and/or father to their children.

Chapter 1
Are Fathers Important?

Yes! Of course fathers are important! But, society wants you to forget the idea of a traditional family with a strong father. Some people have tried to remove or minimize the father's influences from the home and our culture. Television shows that once featured a dominant father as the main character, have now replaced the father with a rebellious youth, who has no regard for family, education, the law, themselves or God!

The old saying, "It takes two to get them, and two to raise them" is rapidly being erased from our culture. Some women believe that they can raise their children without the father's help. Some even feel that, they alone, can teach their sons how to be men. That philosophy is ridiculous, selfish and absolutely WRONG. There's another old saying, "Mothers raise boys, but fathers raise MEN".

The father is the backbone and leader of the family. Prior to an athlete or celebrity, daddy was considered the hero and role model to his children. He was the mechanic, plumber, ATM, counselor, part-time cook, and full-time bodyguard for his family. He impacted many lives within the church and throughout the community. He was known for his physical strength, leadership skills, great wisdom, compassion, and insight.

A father is larger than life in the eyes of his child. A father's presence causes a strong sense of security that comforts a child. When a child is performing in a school activity or sporting event, the father's presence gives the encouragement and confidence his child needs. Even in his discipline, he still shows love. As much as a child needs his (or her) father, a father also needs his child. A father draws strength in investing his knowledge, protection and love into his child.

> *A father's greatest joy is to look into the eyes*
> *of a little person who he helped create.*

Becoming a father for the first time is a life-changing experience. Sometimes, that makes a man prioritize and turn his life completely around. A child can have a magnificent and positive effect in a father's life.

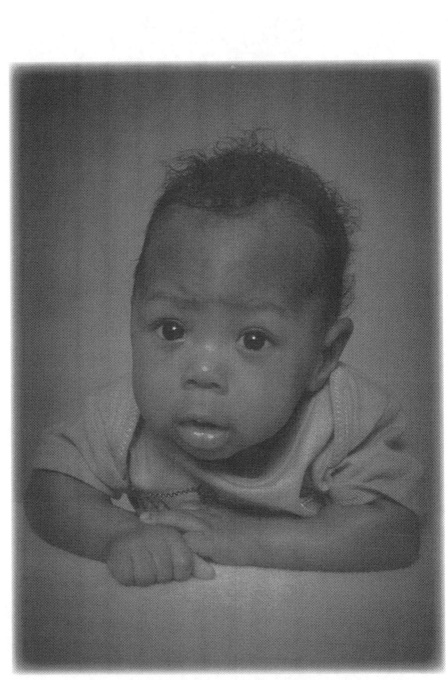

Introducing, Dillon (2006)

Chapter 2
The Origin of Father's Day

Father's Day is set aside for us as a nation to acknowledge who we came from—our fathers. Before we look at the origin of Father's Day, let's compare it to Mother's Day. Mother's Day was first celebrated in 1908; it became a national holiday in 1914.

Although Grace Golden Clayton receives credit for the first Father's Day service on July 5, 1908, it was Sonora Smart Dodd efforts that made it a national holiday. Dodd heard a Mother's Day sermon in 1909 at Central Methodist Episcopal Church. The message inspired her to talk to her pastor about honoring fathers also. Dodd's father, William J. Smart, was a Civil War veteran who raised six children alone after his wife died during child birth. She originally recommended her father's birthday, June 5, but her pastor didn't have enough time to prepare a sermon. The service took place two weeks later on June 19, 1910, at a YWCA in Spokane, Washington.

In 1913, a bill was introduced to make Father's Day nationally known. Three years later, after speaking at a Father's Day service, President Woodrow Wilson wanted to make the holiday official, but Congress continuously refused to do so.

In the 1930's Dodd begin to push for the Father's Day movement again. This time, she had the help of the Father's Day Council, founded by the New York Associated Men's Wear Retailers, the manufacturers of ties, tobacco products and many other companies that would create traditional gifts to fathers.

For years, many people were against the idea of making Father's Day a national holiday, thinking it was copying the commercial success of Mother's Day. In spite of the negative responses and jokes, the Father's Day supporters kept on fighting.

In 1957, Maine Senator Margaret Smith wrote a proposal accusing Congress of honoring mothers and ignoring fathers. In 1966, President Lyndon B. Johnson issued the first presidential proclamation to designate the third Sunday of June as Father's Day. In 1972, President Richard Nixon made it a national holiday when he signed it into law.

Chapter 3
The Meaning of a Father

"He (Cornelius) was a godly man, deeply reverent, as was his entire household. He gave generously to charity and was a man of prayer."

Acts 10:2 The Living Bible

What is the definition of a father?
1. A father is a man who has begotten a child from his own seed (sperm) or through adoption.
2. The Greek word for father is **pater** (Int'l Standard Bible Encyclopedia). It comes from a root word that means "nourisher, protector, and upholder."

The first step in being a good father is being a good man! One must function as a mature, responsible male; thinking, acting and operating maturely. A male of good morals and ethics. It is often said that some fathers need to step up and be men. But how can you expect them to be men when some of them have never been taught how to be a man?

Everyone has his or her own opinion when asked about the definition of a man. Let's get a final and direct answer from our Creator, God, in His Holy Word.

A male who consults, trust and obeys the Lord in the areas of his life.

(As noted from Proverbs 3:5-6, Isaiah 40:30-31, James 1:5, Galatians 5:16-17; Matthew 6:33).

Chapter 4
The Duties of a Father

*If you don't teach your child about God,
you have ultimately failed as a parent!*

God has given fathers the responsibility to be the spiritual educator to their children. That teaching comes from his words, but more importantly, through his actions and his lifestyle. What children see their fathers do has a greater impact in the children's lives than what the fathers say. When children see their fathers living what they say, it encourages the children to pattern themselves after that and proves that Godly living can be done.

Also, God has the father as the first line of defense for his family. Fathers are the spiritual covering and protectors of the family. God will not allow any attacks from the devil to the body (the family), without forewarning the head (the father).

God is sending information to the fathers about the affairs of his family, but he must be in his rightful spiritual position to hear God speak. A father who refuses his spiritual responsibility is like a man who lies in his bed in the middle of the night ignoring the cries of his daughter, who is faced with immediate danger at the hands of intruders. She screams, *"DADDY, DADDY, HELP ME! THEY'RE HURTING ME, DADDY! SAVE ME!!"*

But instead of the father going to save his daughter, he ignores his daughter's cries, saying, "I don't feel like getting out of my bed! I'm too tired to get up!" He's hoping the intruders will stop on their own and go away.

That would be a horrible and inconsiderate father. Children are depending upon their fathers for spiritual directions. God wants the fathers to be in his rightful spiritual position in order to intercede for his family and be the example of Godly living. Remember, your main goal as a father is to introduce your children to their **REAL** father- God!

Chapter 5
You're Just Like Your Daddy

A crowning moment for a little boy is to walk around the house in his daddy's shoes. Although daddy's shoes are too big for the boy's feet, it gives him pride and confidence to put his daddy's shoes on. Boys are convinced that someday they will fit into their daddy's shoes and be just like their daddy.

A major influence children will have in their lives are their fathers. Fathers are responsible to teach their children about their heritage. They also hold the key to how their children view themselves, how they make decisions, as well as their outlook on life. Without the father, a child may miss important tools that will help them develop and prepare for life.

Some fathers have a hard time in their parenting skills and oftentimes it's related to their own upbringing or relationships with their own fathers. Perhaps they are holding on to hurt, unforgiveness or hatred toward their own fathers.

Maybe they have built up anger over the way they were raised, or their fathers were not actively involved in their lives. Possibly, the fathers showed favoritism toward the other siblings, or some men might be disappointed that their fathers didn't measure up to their expectations.

Men who have unforgiveness and bitterness toward their fathers must learn to let the past go. Even if you feel like they don't deserve forgiveness, God requires you to forgive them anyway.

Keep in mind, your father may have done the best he could, with what he knew. If you research your father's upbringing, oftentimes you'll see that he raised you the same way he was raised.

If his father was emotionally distant or detached from his family, your father may have a hard time emotionally connecting or expressing himself with you. If your father was verbally, physically or mentally abusive, there's a great chance that his father was too. When you understand his upbringing, it will help you to have compassion, forgiveness and understanding towards him, instead of hatred. Compassion will help you to break the cycle by offering prayer for him.

Unforgiveness will keep the cycle going and your emotional wounds open for infections! Unforgiveness hurts you instead of the other person. It's just like drinking lethal poison and expecting the other person to die. What you may not realize is, when unforgiveness stays in your heart (spirit), hatred develops. When hatred is in your heart, then oftentimes who you hate, is who you will become.

For example, a young son hates his father for abandoning the family. The son grows up and has a family of his own. As time goes on, that son becomes unfaithful to his wife, has several children from affairs, and then has three failed marriages! He became worse than his father. Even if you didn't respect your father, you MUST respect the authoritative position that he holds! Remember, forgiveness is not just for the other person, but it's for you. Let go of the hatred, repent and allow God to heal you!

Chapter 6
Fathers, Leave Something for Them to Remember You By

When I found out I was going to be a father, my first thought was... *"I AIN'T GOT NO MONEY! HOW IN THE WORLD COULD I BE ABLE TO TAKE CARE OF A CHILD WHEN I COULD BARELY AFFORD MYSELF?"* I thought about all the money I had mismanaged or thrown away. I was thinking, "Oh man! What if my son needs medicine and I can't afford it?" That question made me start saving my money, watch my spending and become more financially responsible for my son's sake. It also prepared me to set an example for him to follow when he becomes of age. I was determined to teach him the value of responsible spending and saving money.

A father must plan ahead for his future and the future of his children. My father used to say, "Save a dry stick for a wet day!" Proverbs 13:22 New King James Version tells us, "A good man leaves an inheritance to his children's children." Think about this! Do you know who your great, great, great, great grand-father is? Many would say, "NO!!!" Do you know why you don't know him? Because, *he didn't leave you nothing*!

If he would've left you with something, he would have been highly discussed when you were growing up. If he was someone like Henry Ford, Sam Walton, Joseph Kennedy, or John Rockerfeller, your family would have a big picture of him displayed in the living room or over the fireplace. Some people think that inheritance only deals with money, but that's not true.

Inheritance also deals with wisdom, moral, character, and ethics. For example, Dr. Martin Luther King Jr. He was not a multi-millionaire or an entertainer. He was a great man who showed Godly strength, compassion, discipline and wisdom. Now, because of what he taught and demonstrated, his children and many others around the world are enjoying the fruits of his labor and keeping his legacy alive!

There's a special feeling about receiving something from your daddy that you hold dear to your heart. I remember my daddy giving me his old hand-me-downs (and very much out-of-style) clothes. But, because the clothes were from my daddy, I placed great value on them. Every chance I had (Halloween, '70s day at school, etc.), I'd wear one of those old outfits. Regardless if they were torn or full of holes, I didn't throw them away, because my daddy gave them to me. What mattered to me was not what I received, but who I received it from - **MY DADDY**!

Daddy (1983)

Chapter 7
The Man and His Loins

Here's something to think about-the seed of a man is highly important! Sin has always been seen as passing from a father to a child, not through a mother (Deuteronomy 5:9; Exodus 20:5, 34:7; Numbers 14:18; Leviticus 26:39-40; Hebrews 7:9-10).

The Bible traces human reproduction to women without sinful responsibility of passing from a mother to a child. This is how Jesus could be born of a virgin woman, and still not be sinful flesh. (Matthew 1:18-23; Luke 1:32-35; Romans 8:3; Galatians 4:4). Also realizing, a father can pass down blessings or curses to his offspring, even while they are still in a father's loins! Hebrews 7:9-10 tells us that Levi paid tithes while still in (his father's) Abraham's loins.

An Example of Exposing Your Seeds to Wickedness:
If you go to a strip club, not only are you giving yourself permission to go, but you're also giving permission to your seeds (children). You allow demonic spirits associated with strip clubs, such as pornography, prostitution, rape, alcoholism, and drug abuse to be passed down to your seeds and their descendants. Since you are carrying your seeds inside your loins, your children and their descendants are with you in whatever bad or good activities or atmosphere you're involved in. Remember, wherever you go, whatever you say, whatever you do, your seeds are with you *all the time.*

Chapter 8
You're Responsible For Your Seed!!

MEN, God had given you the responsibility for your seeds!

I strongly believe that if men knew the value and importance of themselves (and their seeds), they would have avoided a lot of foolish mistakes. Some men have been taught that being a man makes it acceptable to have multiple sexual partners or one-night stands. Others believe that commitment is for a man after he has sown his *"wild oats"*.

If a man was a virgin or abstaining from sex, most people would label him weird, unmanly or gay because of his decision. It is considered abnormal for a man to be a respectable gentleman. A man who understands the value of his seed knows he must study and research the woman he's considering dating and marrying.

Think of it like this: A skilled farmer looks for healthy soil and has it tested to ensure the health of the soil. Good quality soil will give the plant food, water, higher quality results and helps it to grow. A well-drained soil allows oxygen and water to reach the root zone to promote healthy roots.

Well, just like the farmer, a man must carefully study the soil that may possibly receive his seeds. He allows wise counsel to test and observe the woman he sees as his potential mate.

Sometimes wise counsel can pick up on bad character, motives or potential problems that the man inquiring may have overlooked.

A man cannot assume that what he sees or what he hears from the potential mate is all that he needs to know and everything is all out in the open. There is a devil with a planned attack toward him. That's why a man can't plant his seeds in just any woman's soil. It may be bad or contaminated.

Many good men have had *"baby mama drama"* because of the unwise choice of dating, having sex with or marrying the wrong woman. Many good men have been thrown in jails, falsely accused, hurt, or even killed because of their baby mama. God wants the man to understand his value and know that the devil wants to link him with the wrong woman.

Satan wants to eliminate or diminish the man's purpose, reputation, and effectiveness within his family, community, church and country. When a man understands the value of himself and his seed, he'll be more mindful in consulting God for a Godly wife, and in avoiding any pitfalls.

Chapter 9
When Daddy's Away,
The Devil Will Play

WOMEN: You must be careful and mindful of the seeds you allow inserted into your soil!

There are some guys who don't deserve to have a pet hamster, much less a child! When a woman chooses the wrong guy to father her child, she increases the chance of her child growing up fatherless.

According to a 1999 report of the Department of Health and Human Services:

"A girl without a father in her life is 2 1/2 times as likely to get pregnant and 53% more likely to commit suicide. A boy without a father in his life is 63% more likely to run away and 37% more likely to abuse drugs."

The following are recent statistics about children of divorce and separation from the newsletter Common Sense & Domestic Violence, 1998 01 30:

63% of youth suicides are from fatherless homes. [U. S. D.H.H.S. Bureau of the Census]

90% of all homeless and runaway children are from fatherless homes.

85% of all children that exhibit behavioral disorders come from fatherless homes. [Center for Disease Control]

80% of rapist motivated with displaced anger come from fatherless homes. [Criminal Justice and Behavior, Vol. 14 p. 403-26]

71% of all high school dropouts come from fatherless homes. [National Principals Association Report on the State of High Schools]

70% of juveniles in state operated institutions come from fatherless homes [U.S. Dept. of Justice, Special Report, Sept., 1988]

85% of all youths sitting in prisons grew up in a fatherless home. [Fulton County Georgia Jail Populations and Texas Dept. of Corrections, 1992]

Chapter 10
Daddy Versus the System

Fathers: Do not allow the law, the courts, baby mama, or any other situation define who you are as a father or as a man. Some people are quick to call certain fathers *"deadbeat dads"*. But, when the judicial system is keeping them down, the baby mamas are lying on them, and when it appears that the weight of the world is on their shoulders, no one acknowledges them as *"beat down dads"!* There is a negative stigma attached to a man who is no longer romantically involved with his child's mother - even if she's at fault. A father shouldn't be punished or treated unfairly because the relationship ended.

Father: Do not allow the media, the law, the baby's mother, or another man's situations make you give up doing what's right towards your child. It is easy to get discouraged when you're doing what's right, yet the courts and everyone else are siding against you. Don't respond to their foolishness! If there are any mistreatments you receive from your children's mother, remember to document everything that is done (with dates and times).

Do not assume that things or details are not important enough to document. That very thing you think is unimportant may be the very thing to help the case turn in your favor. Focus on being the adult and bigger person in the matter! Trust God in knowing that He sees everything and has a deadline for your injustice.

In some cases, fathers who do not have their children living with them have a legal court-ordered arrangement for visitation with their children.

Do your very best to stick with your visitation time and try not to break any visits. If you cannot make your visitation time, please be honest with your child and their mother. Make sure it's for a legitimate reason. Don't make a habit of breaking your commitments. It will ultimately break the trust your child has towards you.

Some fathers don't know how to handle being away from their child. A good suggestion would be to seek a professional Christian counselor or a trusting pastor. Also, create a daily journal to your child. Write down your thoughts, hopes, and dreams for them. Be very open and honest, but please, filter it with wisdom.

Do not write anything negative about work or the child's mother or her family. Also, if you're active in church and can't be present with your child, do not use church as an excuse. The devil could use that to make the child resent church or God.

If you have multiple children, get a journal for each child. If a child has his or her own journal, it will acknowledge them as their own individual and it will be more personable. Even if they never read it, it may be very therapeutic for you.

Chapter 11
The Heart of a Man

Most men will acknowledge their mistakes, but they won't acknowledge their hurts!

The reason is... Hurt exposes the heart. Society says that it's acceptable for women to open up and express their feelings, but it's unacceptable and forbidden for men to express theirs. Men have emotions, fears and concerns too. Some people feel that only weak or feminine type men open up their hearts or express their feelings. Actually, it takes a self-confident man to express his feelings and emotions in-spite of potential criticism.

The role that best describes the heart of a good man is... The role of a pastor. A pastor is the spiritual dad who has the responsibility to be a leader, mentor and confidant to many. They show selfless action of love. Genuine pastors are on call 24 hour a day, 7 days a week, to meet the needs, concerns and welfare of others, regardless if they're the pastor's members or not. When a person is hurting, a true pastor feels the hurt as well. Just like a pastor, a good man has a heart for God and people.

Five natural impulses of a good man's heart. His heart will protect, provide, serve, supply chivalry and encourage.

PROTECT

Men were built to protect and cover the family. Although some men are taught how to protect, others are instinctive protectors, especially to those who they care for. They are concerned about every aspect of those who are close to their hearts. To protect a man's heart, he will protect those who are near to his heart. Some men would risk their own lives, for the safety of the family. As protective as men are about the families' physical safety, they are equally concern about the families' emotional safety.

When most fathers see their child cries (especially a daughter), those fathers want to seek revenge towards whoever hurt their child. The need to protect his children is important to the father and most feel that it defines their role as a father.

The father covers the family spiritually too. He leads or oversees prayer and Bible study at home. He studies each child to learn their individual spiritual gifts and personalities. The father teaches the family the need to rely and trust God in every area of life.

<u>PROVIDE</u>

Most men want to be the bread winners in the homes. They want to ensure that they supply the needs of the family with little to no help from others. Some would consider that being a provider defines who they are as men. Those men would go without things to make sure the family needs were met.

There have been many stories of fathers walking to work, skipping lunch, getting a second or third job to ensure the needs of the family were met. When the family needs are met, his needs are met.

One of the most difficult days in a father's life is to walk his daughter down the aisle and hand her over to her soon to be husband. The father is concern if his soon to be son-in law could provide for his daughter just as he did. Most fathers have a hard time emotionally letting go of their daughters.

Even if their daughters are adults, most dads still see their daughters as the pony tail wearing, knee high socks wearing, little innocent daddy's girl, with an adorable smile, in need of her daddy's protection and provision.

SERVICE

This is the time for most men to shine, because it showcases the opportunity to build or fix something, to mentor, teach, or give some advice to those they love.

As a father: In some homes, fathers have been the parent to give their children driving lessons, teaching the children how to ride bikes and how to catch a ball. Those were labeled as ***Daddy duties***. It serves as a time when fathers bond with their children. Those memories will remain within the children's heart, for a lifetime.

As a husband: Most wives look forward to this type of heart impulse. They refer to this as the ***honey do's***. If something is broken and needs to get fixed, it goes on the honey do's list. If the wife wants the house painted, the garage cleaned, errands ran or something picked up from a store, it would all be placed on the honey do's list. Some husbands' vacation is not spent sitting at home relaxing or watching TV. It's spent working on all the chores on the honey do's list, to keep the wife happy.

A form of service that some men don't do very well in is… **Conversation**. Most women like to engage into stimulating verbal dialogs in person or by phone that's more personal than texting. Although it takes little physical effort, it's one of the hardest things for some men to do. Unlike some women who go into lengthier, detailed conversations, most men are straight forward, get to the point talkers. Less is more is most men's concept. Sometimes men are horrible with verbal communication because they may not find the exact words that properly express how they feel or what they say may not come out the way they desired.

Most husbands make-up for their lack of conversation skills and earn some major *brownie points* by… **Listening to her talk**. Most women loves a man who would listen to them. It makes them feel important and valuable. They feel that if a man effectively listens to them, he cares. It builds her confidence in him and draw them closer together in their relationship.

Some men understand that if his wife wants to tell him how bad her day was, **DON'T INTERRUPT**! It may be an opportunity for him to serve her by fixing the problem and be looked upon as her knight and shining armor. He wants to come to her rescue.

He believes that when a woman tells a man about a problem, the man supposed to take the initiative to fix it without the woman asking him to. He works all day and night to fix the problem, until he finishes. He is excited because he thinks he's helping her by fixing it. What's interesting is, some women would question him on why he fixed it. She later informs him that she told him because she needed to vent. That drives a man crazy!

From his perspective, why bring it up if you didn't want it fixed? Also, a problem that's addressed is no longer an issue, if it's fixed! He fixed the problem, but his work was unappreciated! Although he may be disappointed at the outcome, he does not regret his actions. If he realizes that his assistance would help his spouse, he would do it again.

CHIVALRY

Chivalry is NOT dead! It's in the heart of those referred to as... **GENTLEMEN**! The Merriam-Webster Dictionary defines chivalry as: Behaving in an honorable or polite way, showing respect and politeness especially toward women. Gentlemen understand the importance of chivalry in a romantic relationship. Here are a few things that gentlemen do:

- ✓ Open and hold the door for a woman
- ✓ Pull a chair out at a table for a woman
- ✓ Lift or carry somethings for a woman
- ✓ Hold the hands of their mate
- ✓ Give public affection
- ✓ See to it that a woman doesn't stand or wait alone
- ✓ When walking with his mate, walk near the curb of a street.
- ✓ Help a woman with her coat or offering her his coat
- ✓ Stand up as she walks into a room
- ✓ As a father: A father teaches his son how *TO SERVE* his future wife and the daughter how *TO BE SERVED* as a future wife.
- ✓ When a father teaches his son chivalry, it teaches his son how to treat and respect women and helps him to be the ideal husband.

Chivalry helps his daughter to maintain a healthy self-esteem and self-awareness of who she is. When a father gives her chivalry, it helps her to seek that kind of man who would give her those kind of treatments and what kind of husband she deserves.

Although the father displays chivalry towards his daughter, when his son demonstrates it towards his sister, it reinforces to her, the character of a loving, caring man and help the son to find a future wife who welcomes his chivalry services. Chivalry amongst children bonds the family closer together.

When the family is traveling together, the father opens his daughter's door, but leave to go open his wife's door and assists her out the car. It teaches his daughter to expect a guy to open the door, but the ONLY ONE who should have the honor of assisting her out the car, is someone who has earned and proven himself to be her potential spouse.

As a husband: Chivalry keeps the intimacy and romance levels high within the marriage. It keeps the marriage exciting. It reaffirms the love the husband have for his wife.

ENCOURAGEMENT

Words of encouragement are good to hear from neighbors, friends, even your own mother, but there's something special and fulfilling about receiving it from your daddy that is unmatched by anyone else. Most children seek the approval of their dads. It doesn't matter how a child does in a recital class, during a baseball game, or spelling bee, if daddy is pleased, no one else's opinion matters.

I remember as a kid, I played the trombone horn. I had to practice with a house full of siblings who always told me to give up playing or that I was a horrible trombone player. One winter school night, I was practicing my trombone. My siblings had enough of my playing. While my daddy was laying hot asphalt in the backyard, they all went to get him, so he could tell me to stop playing because it was late and I played horribly.

My siblings followed my daddy into my bedroom where I was practicing. My daddy turned to my siblings and said, "If you all don't like his playing, all of you all can stand outside in the cold, until he's finished!" My siblings took daddy's advice and went to the backyard, in the cold weather and stood on hot asphalt! What a load of confidence and encouragement that was for me from my daddy! He stood up for me and encouraged me to never give up.

My father is known as a great encourager. If someone was feeling low or questioning their abilities, he would say the right things to help them get back on focus. Although my father had limited education, there were many people with higher education than my father called him for his insight and advice.

My father was not only a great encourager, he was a great supporter. Growing up, I use to get an allowance of $5 a week. While most of the kids were buying candies, junk food or toys, I would get my allowance and give it to my cousins so I could play the drums at church. My daddy found out about it and gave me $5 for my allowance and another $5 for me to give to my cousins, so I could play the drums. Although I did not sound good to many (especially to my sister Sheila), my daddy would sit at the church pulpit with a smile and give me a thumbs up!

Children can be more successful in achieving their goals and dreams with the support of their father than those who did not receive support from their fathers.

Chapter 12
What He Really Wants is…
RESPECT

A man's ultimate desire is to receive respect, especially from his own family. Respect is the fabric of a man! It gives a man security, his identity, and worth. He thirsts for her attention. A man does not want his spouse to do more for others than for him! For a man, respect is as important as life itself. Just as a human being inhales oxygen to live and exhales carbon dioxide, men survive on or inhale respect.

When a person exhales on or talks to a flower, the flower grows. The flower grows because it thrives on what the human is exhaling… carbon dioxide. The human exhales carbon dioxide, the flower inhales it, the flower exhales oxygen and the human inhales it. When a man receives or inhales respect, he releases or exhales love. The woman will inhale love and exhale respect. Love is the man's response towards receiving or inhaling respect.

It is important for a man to choose a woman who is capable of exhaling respect. If he seeks someone who is broken, unhealed or wounded, she is holding her emotional breath and unable to exhale, respond or supply to him the oxygen (respect) he needs.

Along with checking her emotional health, it's important to analyze her maturity level.

Understand that you are choosing your child's potential stepmother. Know that if she's immature and you and her relationship is rocky and troublesome, the relationship between her and your child may be worse. Make sure you choose someone who wants to be with you ***and*** *your child!* Remember, you are not a package deal, because packages can be broken or altered. Instead, you are a combo deluxe, because you have great value that can't be separated or diminished and will benefit whoever claims you. ***Understand that your child's future and happiness are dictated by this important decision.***

Respect is the heartbeat of a man. When a man feels respected by a woman, it will make him walk through a fiery wall for her. A man will give a woman almost anything when she shows him respect. 1 Peter 3:6, describes Sarah respect for Abraham and how she referred to him as "lord". This was not meant to show Sarah inferiority. In that culture, the word lord signified respect. Sarah's respect for Abraham was matched by his love for her. Chapter five in the Book of Ester recounts how she risked her life by approaching the king. But because she used wisdom and respect in dealing with him, the king spared Ester's life, along with the lives of the Jews.

Chapter 13
The Step Daddy

In closing, I want to acknowledge a special group of men-- stepdads, or in some cases, the *"step-up"* dads. For some children, *"step-up"* dads fill the voids left by the biological fathers' absence or noninvolvement with their children.

Stepdads have chosen a path that is unpopular and oftentimes unappreciated. A biological father doesn't choose his child. On the other hand, a *"step-up"* dad has a choice; he accepts responsibilities and welcomes the circumstances that come with the child, the child's mother and in some cases, the biological father.

He has a lot at risk, because he welcomed the child, but there's no guarantee that the stepdad would be welcomed by the child. Being a stepdad is more than a title or position, *it's a ministry*! It requires a lot of prayer, patience, discernment, wisdom, and love as a stepdad to help the family blend together properly. It's important for him to be before God in prayer for direction in how to raise his new family.

I used to wonder if anyone in the Bible could relate to being a stepdad. God led me to Mary's husband Joseph in Matthew 1:18-25 and Luke 2:41-52. When he learned Mary was pregnant, he chose to marry her anyway.
When Jesus was 12 years old, away from his family, his mother asked him, "Where were you?" Jesus said, "I was about my father's business!" In the midst of knowing that Jesus was not referring to him, Joseph taught Jesus about carpet therefore Jesus was known as the carpenter's son. Jesus outcome displayed Joseph's influence and care for Jesus. Joseph set a great example of the ministry of being a stepdad. Joseph was the ultimate stepdad.

Chapter 14
The Charge to Fathers

Here is my challenge to the fathers:

Examine your role as a father. Is God pleased? Are you giving your child your very best? Ask yourself this: If you had a daughter marrying a guy just like you, would you be happy with her choice she's making? If your answer is no, this is your time to go to God and confess your sins and shortcomings. Receive His forgiveness and accept Him as your Savior.

If you're tired of pretending that all is well when you're really hurting or scared, Jesus is here to help you! If you're tired of being successful outside the house but failing inside the house, will you come to God? Know that you will not be successful relying on your own strength or abilities. You must allow God to help you be the father He wants you to be. Know, it's not too late to start your new life! Your family is cheering for you! **YOU CAN DO IT!!**

To the mothers/daughters: If you're a single mother who has unforgiveness, anger or hurt in your heart because of your child's father or your father, will you tell God all about your hurt and disappointments?

Matthew 11:28 "Come unto Me, all you who labor and are heavy laden, and I will give you rest.

29) Take My yoke upon you, and learn from Me, for I am gentle and lowly in heart, and you will find rest for your souls.
30) For My yoke is easy, and My burden is light."

Matthew 11:28-30 (New King James Version)

Chapter 15
A Prayer to the Fathers

Dear Heavenly Father,

I come to you thanking you for being a faithful, loving, Holy God. I ask you to forgive me for all my sins. I receive your forgiveness and thank you for your forgiveness. Lord! I am in desperate need of you in my life! My ways have gotten me into problems and situations YOU didn't plan for me to have.

I apologize if I mismanaged or played with any woman's heart! Remove every soul tie from me and break every generational curse that is over or in me! Cleanse me from any resentment I may have towards my father, my child's mother or myself! I release all pain, hurt, anger and unforgiveness in me! I receive YOUR healing, forgiveness and your peace in my life.

Give me the patience and skill to handle any communication and misunderstanding. Help me to operate in love! Help me to be an example of YOU to my kid(s). God! I can NOT do this of my own strength or ability. You have permission to take complete control of my life! Give me your wisdom and discernment for my life! I need your guidance in my life! Teach me how to be the father after YOUR OWN heart.

Teach me how to love. Teach me to be a man of integrity, character and morals. I bind the work of satan, IN THE NAME OF JESUS! I cancel the devil's plan! I thank you God for the joy, peace, healing and victory you have given me! Thank you for working everything out for my good! I give you the praise, the glory and the honor! In JESUS' NAME… AMEN!!!

Chapter 16
Things You Need to Know

Things you need to know in the unfortunate chance that you divorce or separate from your child's mother:

DO YOUR HOMEWORK

Never rely on someone to do it for you. No one understands the importance of your situation better than you. No one will have the same drive and passion to gather information better than you. It is not anyone else's child at stake- IT'S YOURS! You can find and have your questions answered when you do your own research.

You don't want to put your future and your child's future in the hopes that someone will have your (and your child's) best interest in mind! Even if you have a great attorney, STILL do your research, ask many questions, and create scenarios. You don't want to be unprepared. Equip yourself with as much information as possible!

SPEAK UP FOR YOURSELF

When you allow others to speak on your behalf (other than an attorney), you handicap yourself and become dependent upon others to be your voice. No matter how long it takes, how many words you stumble over, take your time and verbalize your situation.

HIRE YOUR OWN ATTORNEY

There have been couples who tried to take the cheaper route by hiring one attorney to defend both, then in the end, one of them gets *"short changed"* (you can assume which one that would be)! It may cost a little more money up front to hire your own attorney, but you will have your own representative who has your and your child's best interest in mind.

Make sure whatever agreement you have with your child's mother is in writing. Without proper documentation, the agreed upon arrangement may not be legally recognized. You must treat this situation like a business.

NEVER ASSUME ANYTHING

Make sure all communication is clear and understood. If there is something you're unsure of, don't guess or assume that it will be like a previous situation. *Always ask questions* in order to prevent misunderstandings or conflict to help maintain open lines of communication between you and your child's mother.

Understand that child custody is totally different than visitation rights.

Child custody refers to the financial responsibility for the child. Joint custody means both parents share equal financial responsibility, such as splitting the child's medical bills.

Visitation rights deal with you being able to see your child. For parents, if you can create an agreeable schedule amongst yourselves, please do so.

If you're unable to reach an agreement, this results in standard visitation rights. For example, in the state of Texas, the standard visitation is every Thursday from 6-8 p.m. and every other weekend. As you can see, the state will not offer you much and you cannot effectively raise your child with two hours a day, once a week. Visitation rights vary by state so, consult legal advice where you live.

Chapter 17
Words of Encouragement

DEALING WITH CONFLICT

Sometimes you have to laugh to keep from crying, remain silent to avoid saying something that you would regret, or walk away so you won't catch a court case. Regardless of your past or present situations, God is here to give you the strength and wisdom to go through and overcome it all.

You're not defined by the circumstances you're facing, what your enemies say about you or your income, but you're defined by your response to it! Just remember, God can and will bless you in spite of the foolishness or hatred *around you*. Just make sure that it's not *within you!*

In room temperature, water is liquid. In freezing temperature, water becomes ice. In boiling temperature, water becomes gas or vapor. But no matter what the conditions are, the formula for water (H_2O) never changes. With that being said, no matter what condition you're facing, NEVER change your character or formula. Be consistent in who you are in any temperature and your life will be less stressful.

You don't have to attend every argument you're invited to.

When you're in a conflict, tell the devil, "Due to my lack of funds, I will not be paying you attention!" You must increase your prayer life's bank account to bankrupt your attention to the devil's tactics.

If it seems that someone wants to be confrontational - instead of trying to prove a point, or making time for an argument - take a break, pray and regroup.

IN TIMES OF TROUBLE

If it's OUTSIDE of your control, it's INSIDE of God's control. No matter the situation, you are equipped for it. Complain less and trust more that God will fix the problem. He will do what He said!

Your current problem is smaller compared to the past problems God had delivered you from! Trust that God has not forgotten about you, so don't forget about His past victories in your life.

You can't tell Jesus to "*Take the wheel*" when you want to control the brakes. Jesus will not take you through something He didn't prepare or equip you for! Trust that He will change your situation, ONCE and FOR ALL! Trust God and not your own abilities!

If you want to see the hand of God move in your situation, get your hands out of the way.

Although the times of trouble seem uncomfortable, they are the PERFECT opportunities to learn the characteristics (Nature) of God! Whatever area the devil is fighting you in, represents the character he wants to prevent you from knowing about GOD. For marital problems - Jehovah-Shalom / Lord of Peace; health issues - Jehovah- Rophi / God who heals; being in lack- Jehovah- Jireh / God is Provider. Allow times of trouble to reveal the nature of Almighty God.

The rainbow must be introduced by the storm! Don't focus on the announcement called the storm when God brought you to the performance to see the rainbow-your blessing (*dropping the mic on the devil's head*)!

> *In times of trouble, the strength of a man does not come*
> *from the bending of iron, but the bending of his knees!*

If Jesus held His head up on the cross, so can you! His source of strength did not come from His circumstances, but His focus on God the Father. Your victory, or deliverance, begins when your head is up. Look up to the hills from which cometh your help. Your help comes from the Lord.

DEALING WITH UNREASONABLE PEOPLE

The most effective way of dealing with an unreasonable person is to deal with the one in the mirror and allow God to deal with the other person.

> *Don't allow a person's reaction to become your*
> *distraction! Stay focused on your assignment!!*

In an argument, the person who passes on having the last word is the first to receive peace. Don't feel like choosing to remain silent will make you become or appear weak. Those who can't or won't guard their tongues are! Not everything a person says needs a response! To be effective, allow God to give you the patience and wisdom to know what to say, how to say it, and when to say it!

Even if your motives are pure, always consult God on when to talk to a person about an issue. Let God set the groundwork and it will be effective. Wait for God's instructions and you will be successful.

Forgive those who are difficult, as GOD has forgiven that person who was (and sometimes is) difficult.... YOU!

When a home invasion is reported, investigators check the front door to see if there was forced entry. If the door has been damaged, that means the intruders imposed their will upon the homeowner. But if there's no damage to the door, the investigators will determine that the homeowner invited them into the home. When you are upset with someone, remember that they didn't make you mad - you allowed them to make you mad. No one has control of your will or emotions! No one has access into your emotional door unless you invite them in! Pray and ask God to help you to not allow people access into your emotional house. The only house that does not need a welcome mat.

Remember, the next time someone drives you crazy, ask yourself, "Did I give them the keys to drive?"

When you're dealing with unreasonable folks, never step outside of your character. If you do so, you are no longer covered by the radar that insures God to come to your rescue. Your Godly character is the flagship to your victory. Don't take down your flag for any reason or anyone! Let God's Word be your anchor and grip as the winds of life blow and watch GOD tell your storm.... "Peace, be still!"

When it comes to unreasonable people, love the Hell out of them, and the Christ into them.

FEELING ALONE OR REJECTED

When you don't believe that Jesus can forgive you of your past or heal you from emotion pain, you're actually saying, "What Jesus did on the cross, is not enough to cover my sins, hurt, or pain!" The Bible says that Jesus bore every sin for *(Say your name out loud)*! Jesus finished it all on the cross. He rose with all power in His hands. Jesus reconciled us with God, the Father.

We have the confidence to go before Him knowing that we are completely forgiven and He wants to commune with us. No amount of work you can or will do, equals to what Jesus did for *(Say your name out loud)!* Go into God's open, loving, forgiving arm. It's ok! He knows your story - now listen to His story.

A young boy applied for a job he wanted badly. He filled out an application every week for six months. Every time he went, the staff would tell him to keep applying. After the sixth month, the supervisor finally told him he was unqualified for the position and advised him to look for a less demanding job. That rejection devastated the young boy. But on the same day, another job he applied for called him back and eventually hired him.

Some 20+ years later, the young boy is still working there, but the place that rejected him is now out of business. The rejection led him to his God-given purpose. **Sometimes, being rejected is a blessing in disguise!** When you're rejected, it could be the best thing to happen in your life. Sometimes God doesn't allow you to get that job, position, relationship or marriage you desired because, He saw down the road that it was not best for you! Trust and know that God always has your best interest in his heart and has something or someone tailor-made just for you. Be encouraged about God's plan for your life. By the way, that young boy in the story was me. Some of God's great blessings comes from being rejected!

Do not have a guilt trip, pity party, or blame game because the relationship you once had did not last. No matter if they were not the right one, and you ignored the red flags, look at it as a lesson learned and a blessing gained. Reflect on the good times, regardless if the other person contributed to the happiness or not. Make peace with bad decisions, thank God for the experience and forgive yourself from all debts of guilt.

No matter who left you broken in pieces, Jesus came to make you whole, complete and lacking nothing.

As you get closer to your purpose, the devil WILL bring doubt, discouragement, fear and the old feeling of rejection. Remember, the devil knows what's in you and what lies ahead for you. Don't lose focus on the play God gave you. You have a star quarterback in Jesus Christ, the Holy Ghost has your protection and God the Father as the coach, and C.E.O. cheering you on. Victory is yours, but you've got to get in the game!

If misery loves company, don't get upset if people leave your life.

Because a kid throws a baby bottle down, does that mean that milk must change its formula? NO! When that spoil little rascal gets hungry enough, they're gonna realize that temper tantrum made them throw away the best thing they ever had! So regardless of who abandoned you, who broke up with you, who didn't hire you, etc, don't change the formula of who you are! GOD made you with the right ingredients for the right purpose! You changing your formula will distort or contaminate something GOD made good... YOU!

Soon, GOD will place you in the hand of a mate, business, friendship, etc, that will appreciate you and value your formula!

One of the GREATEST blessings God allowed for you was to be REJECTED by others! Such as the job you didn't get, that person who abandoned you, or even your own family who turned their backs on you. The devil thought that those things were going to take you out! But the devil didn't realize God was holding you up all along. Know that everybody who put you down, left you, or talked about you will see you rise up again and take the spot God has made just for you! God will place true, solid people into your life that love you, appreciate you and who aren't trying to use you. You will succeed! I speak the purpose and plan of God for your life! The SAME JESUS who rose from a temporary tomb will raise you up from your temporary condition and plant you in your permanent position, where you were destined to be!

Although you go to God about your BIG problems, He is just as concerned about your small problems! See, your big issues are not the ones getting to you- it's the multitude of small ones that are overwhelming you! God wants you to give ALL to Him! He is concerned about EVERY AREA of your life! Never feel as if you're bugging Him or getting on His nerves! He loves you so much and wants you to know you excite Him when you go to Him. He loves you and wants you to trust Him with all you have. No longer do you have to think about dealing with things alone! God says, "GIVE IT TO ME!"

FORGIVING YOURSELF

DO NOT beat yourself up or blame yourself about how your children turned out or their mistakes! If you have done all that you could in God's ability, free yourself from all that guilt! Your children have seen an example through you, and they were raised up as they should have been. Understand, they are of age to make their OWN decisions about salvation, life, etc.! The devil wants to stress you out and make you feel that God doesn't care! Take comfort in knowing that God doesn't blame you when you've done your part. Place your children in the Mighty hands of God, receive God's love and live your life... BLAME-FREE!!!

No matter how tough they were, thank GOD for the lessons learned! When you accept the learned lessons, your healing begins (or continues), the root of issues becomes clearer, your stress level lowers and you're placed on the path of GOD'S purpose and blessings over your life!

GOD can put to final rest whatever your past mistakes people try to wake up. Embrace God's complete forgiveness, once and for all!

GOD has forgiven you and others have forgiven you. Now, forgive YOURSELF!!!

Don't allow your past mistakes stop you from your present (or future) mission! Acknowledge it, accept it, & learn from it! Remember the AWESOME POWER of GOD'S FORGIVENESS!!

You can never love someone, until you learn to love yourself.
You can never love yourself until you learn to love GOD.
You can never understand GOD's love, until you forgive those who hurt you (your enemies and yourself)!!

Never go to bed angry at YOURSELF!! You may sabotage your quality of rest (peace), dreams or purpose that GOD has for you. You can't beat yourself up over a decision you regret, when GOD wants you to rest for ANOTHER chance called TOMORROW. Peaceful sleep requires you to forgive others and forgive YOURSELF.

SELF-ESTEEM/ SELF-WORTH

Never concern yourself with people who have their thumbs on you to put you down, when GOD has HIS hands on you to lift you up!!

Psalms 17:8 and Zechariah 2:8 tell you that you are the apple of God's eye! The word apple does not refer to the fruit you eat. It is a metaphor for the pupil of your eye. The original meaning of the word pupil is little doll, or little man. It is referring to the little doll or little man of the eye. That means, when you look into someone's eyes, you see a reflection of yourself (the little doll/man)! That means, when God looks into your eyes, He sees a reflection of Himself.

Also, since you were born, everything on your body has grown, or changed, except for one thing—your eyes. You have the same size eyes you had when you were born as you do now. That means, no matter your past, whatever situations occurred in your life, how others see you, or how you see yourself, God sees the same image of Himself in you now that He saw when you were born. You have no reason to hate yourself or feel little about yourself. You are highly loved, valuable, and tailor-made by God! No matter if you've been told you won't be anything, or that you're too short or ugly, God said, "I made you just how I wanted you. You look like Me, you act like Me. You are the apple of My eyes and when I look into your eyes, I see Myself."

If you build your life based upon other people's opinions, you will have a crooked life!

God hand-crafted you at a carefully-selected time for a divine purpose. There is no one like you. Even identical twins have different fingerprints and D.N.A. Love and embrace the uniqueness of you!

Stop talking negatively about yourself! You're giving permission for others to think and say the same thing about you!

Everything God made was made complete and good! That means God made quality people, with a quality plan, for a quality purpose! That means… You weren't made for nothing! You were made for something awesome!

<u>BROKEN-HEARTED</u>

The way to stop bleeding is to treat the wound. The way to heal your heart is to acknowledge that it's bleeding, so God can heal the wounds! An unhealed heart will bleed to death and kill you and all current and future relationships.

Look into the mirror and tell yourself everything you want to hear others tell you.

After a team loses a games, a good coach would get his team and study each play to see where they went wrong, and how to prevent the same mistake from happening again. That's the same principle you must do after the ending of a failed or unsuccessful relationship! You must be mature and responsible enough to examine the past relationships and learn from it! Don't beat yourself up over past mistakes, don't live in regret, but offer forgiveness and peace to your past! GOD wants you to learn from your past, so you can have a successful relationship! GIVE YOURSELF PERMISSION TO LOVE AGAIN!!

Regardless who leaves you, NEVER leave YOURSELF!!!

You MUST learn to laugh at pain! Laughing during the pain takes the lethal venom out of the devil's bite, so it won't infect your heart! In times of pain, sadness, heartbreak, or disappointments, give God your hurt as He gives you your healing through your laughter!

It doesn't make you less than a Christian to admit that you're hurting!

48

As a child, you dreamt of love, marriage, commitment. Now, as an adult, you have given up on love and settled for lust, being a friend with benefits, because your heart has been broken too many times. So many people STOP loving and living because of how their heart was treated in the past. As bad as your heart hurts, and you say you'll never love again, deep within your heart, you desire that TRUE LOVE with the RIGHT person! Look, ALL men aren't dogs, and ALL women don't play games. Don't let the experience of your past kill the dreams of your youth. TRUE LOVE STILL EXIST. Give GOD ALL the hurt, broken dreams, disappointments, and pain. HE will renew, refresh, and revive you and your dreams. Allow HIM to guide you to where love knows no hurt. Trust GOD guidance and receive the TRUE LOVE... AT LAST.

Just because you prayed that you two would get back together and you all didn't, doesn't mean that GOD doesn't love you or that HE doesn't want you married. GOD knows that you love with ALL your heart, and that person was NOT going to put into the relationship what you put in. Know that GOD hadn't forgotten about you or your desire for love and marriage. True romance STILL exist and GOD got you on HIS list for it. #Praise GOD for your Tailor-Made Love.

Don't cry over someone who didn't sweat or work to get you. THAT DEVIL IS A LIAR. Pick yourself up, love on yourself, and be ready for someone who will work to get you, work to keep you and appreciate having you.

There is NO hurt that GOD CAN'T heal!!!!

Don't allow someone to make you feel like your life will fall apart without them. Don't accept that physical, emotional or mental abuse. As GOD as your foundation, you WILL be fine without them. Let them see that the door swings both way: When they leave OUT, GOD will bring the RIGHT one IN. You deserve BETTER!!

<u>GUARDING YOUR HEART</u>

Just because you forgave someone does NOT mean that you have to automatically trust them. Forgiveness cleanse you mentally, emotional, and spiritually; it prevents you from being trapped by hatred and bitterness in your heart. Regardless of a person's attitude or behavior, forgiveness is mainly for you! Trust, on the hand, MUST BE EARNED, NOT GIVEN. If someone violates your trust, it's THEIR responsibility to earn it back, NOT yours to automatically give it! Don't allow anyone to make you feel guilty because you are guarding yourself. It does NOT make you less than a Christian to make someone work for your trust. Even the Bible encourages you to lay hands suddenly on NO one (1 Timothy 5:22- That means don't automatically give your trust away. Allow them to prove themselves). Use GODLY wisdom when you're dealing with folks & your heart will be protected.

Don't give V.I.P. seats to someone who didn't
appreciate being in general admission!

Don't confuse chivalry with common courtesy. Sure it's good for a guy to open the door for a woman or for a woman to tell a guy thank you. Those are kind gestures. You can't truly know or judge a person's character by those things. The only way to know them is to discern their motives (intentions) and true identity. Allow GOD to reveal the red flags or green lights on the streets of LOVE. And don't forget to ask HIM to help you ACCEPT what HE reveals to you.

Love and trust must be earned and proven to qualify for your heart. Give people the benefit of the doubt when they give you proof of their honesty and integrity.

Your love has to be EARNED, not GIVEN!!

Let God have your heart and ask HIM who should get visitation rights. If you can't trust a person before marriage, marrying them will not make them trustworthy. A person's words say who they want you to think they are, but a person's actions say who they really are.

Don't make heart decisions with your heart - make heart decisions with your HEAD. Your heart is to be protected. Your heart is inside of a cage called the **RIB CAGE**. Your head has all your senses. Your head is the armed guard protecting the valuable gift inside the cage called... **YOUR HEART**. Use your head by consulting with God the Father and your heart will be in safe hands.

To know the value of your heart, you MUST know and understand the value of your words. Guard your heart by filtering the words you say to people.

Don't pack your past baggage into your future's luggage!

GRIEF

For those who are grieving or missing a loved one, reflect on the happy times that brought you joy. Remember the wisdom that was imparted. Honor their legacy that they held so true. No longer feel that you didn't tell them enough or show them enough of how much you cared! Rest in knowing that they transcended knowing that what you invested was more than enough to carry them throughout eternity and that they knew how much you love them! Celebrate today.

May God comfort you! Know that you never lose someone when you KNOW where they are. They are in our hearts and in our memories. Also, with the effects their lives have on others, the results keep them alive FOREVER. Their LEGACY lives on, in our lives and in our hearts.

You are lifted up in prayer. It doesn't make you weak or less than a Christian to grieve. Not only is it healthy, but the BIBLE encourages you to grieve. Know, GOD will give you the strength and comfort you need to make it through. GOD promise you that HE will never leave or abandoned you. That is not only in times of trouble, but in times of grieve. As valuable as your loved one was to you, you were that (and more) to them! Today, reflect on the happy times, laugh at the silly times, and honor their legacy throughout the day.

Every emotion that you feel, Jesus understand! No longer feel that you have no one who understands…. JESUS UNDERSTANDS.

Don't let anyone tell you how to grieve. There is no set steps or specific order to follow. Give yourself permission to deal with it as you go. Understand, this is a daily journey for the rest of your life. Know that you're not alone on this journey, Jesus is with you at every step. When you feel like you can't go on, His arms are strong and wide enough to carry you the rest of the way through.

Death is not the end of a person! The word death simple means separation from this earthly life. Death is not a period in a person's life. It is a comma, because it's leading to a new beginning and meaning… From mortality to immortality.

Jesus' death defeated death so that we could have eternal life!!

GETTING YOUR LIFE BACK

What do Superman, Batman, Wonder Woman and Spiderman all have in common? Besides being superheroes, they were ordinary people who had a normal life outside of their superhero duties. No matter what "superhero" title you carry (C.E.O., pastor, officer, parent, minister, etc), you **must** realize that you're STILL a human being and in a human body that depends on rest, relaxation, and a social life.

You can't do it all by yourself. God wants you to have a healthy balance in your life. You *must* learn to delegate responsibilities to others, you *must* take care of yourself by eating right, getting quality rest, getting away at times, and socializing with other people (social events).

Sometimes you have to turn down requests or tell people "No, I can't do it." So, don't let people put guilt trips on you. Running around thinking you're helping the world, but losing your home, family or killing yourself "trying" to run to the rescue for able-bodied people was *not* God's intent for you.

God wants you refreshed, regrouped, revived, and relaxed for the assignment and responsibilities He has for you, but you won't be effective if your fuel is on "E" mentally, emotionally, financially, and even spiritually. Grandparents, let your kids raise *their own* kids. Bosses, make the workers do their *own* jobs. Parents, stop trying to *re-raise* grown folks. Pastors, don't let grown folks take you to an early grave. Remove your superhero uniform when you're *not* on duty and enjoy God, your life, and all that God created just for you. Life's ultimate purpose and fulfillment is to please God - not man.

It's healthy to say, *"NO"*. Saying no will set up your boundaries and you'll be least likely to be taken advantage of. Don't let anyone make you feel bad for saying no. You *must* stick to *your* decision of saying no. The power to say no does not belong to anyone else but *you*.

WAITING/BUILDING PATIENCE

I went to my car to start it. Then, I turned the car off to run back into the house. When I returned to my car, my car would not start. All my lights flashed until I unplugged the battery. Right before I was going to blame the devil, God told me He *allowed* it to happen. God told me to consider the fact that I was at home. Then HE told me that HE didn't want me stranded at work or on the road because I was going to get my son after work. HE told me to go back into the house, study His Word until a repair shop opens. In other words, God told me to WAIT until where He wants me to be at, was available. Stressing was not going to fix the car, but instead it would only get me distracted and keep me dwelling on the problem. As I prayed and studied, the person I was going to call to help me, was touched by God to call and tell me they were coming by. Trust that, if you're in God's hands, know and believe that your plans are there too. Waiting is NOT a punishment instead it's a privilege to see Almighty God flex His muscles by orchestrating something that will leave you breathless.

When your preparation meets your purpose, GOD grants you your promotion to your destination!

A red traffic light signals you to stop to allow those traveling in the opposite direction to proceed. You must wait for your light to turn green for you to move ahead. When you run a red light, you are in violation and could have an accident, get a ticket or be placed under arrest. When God has you waiting for something, you must wait until He gives you the spiritual green light. Running God's spiritual red light could make you crash and ruin your blessing, place you under a spiritual arrest, holdup, detain or forfeit your blessing. Wait for God's timing for what you're trusting and believing Him for.

STOP PANICKING! GOD HASN'T FORGOTTEN ABOUT YOU. HE'S WORKING BEHIND THE SCENE and ABOUT TO START THE SHOW. JUST REMAIN SEATED!!!

The reason why nice guys (or girls) finish last is they're running the wrong race trying to achieve the wrong prize. Never change who you are to go after something or someone who was NOT meant for you (relationships, careers, positions). Go for things (or people) who will celebrate you, not tolerate you. Matthew 6:33 tells you that when you seek 1st the Kingdom of GOD and HIS righteousness (GOD's way of doing the right thing), then all these things will chase you down. You won't have to look for your blessings. Your blessings will be looking for you!

Don't get upset or worry when things aren't happening in your timing. Remember, it's within GOD's timing. Adjust your watch to HIS clock and you'll NEVER be late!

You're too close to give up! You're closer to the finish line than the starting line! Hang in there! GOD will carry you through!

A SPECIAL LETTER TO MY SON

Dillon,

I want to take the time to say that Daddy loves you and is very proud of you! You are a great son and I appreciate you dearly! I am a blessed man to be your father and look forward to seeing you grow into an awesome man of God! Before you were born, the doctors were concerned that you were going to have health issues. As I begin to pray, God showed me a vision of you as a powerful teenager in the Lord! That image of you never left me. Every day I see you, you are becoming more and more of that person in that vision!

My oath is to be the example of a real man of God for you! Not just with words, but with my actions! I pray that God orders your every step and covers you with His wisdom, discernment, and love! I pray that God blesses you to be the husband and father after His heart. God will lead you to a beautiful wife that will always honor, respect, and love you.

I bind every way the devil may try to derail you from God's plan and purpose. I speak joy, peace, victory, healing and favor in your life, IN THE NAME of JESUS! My personal oath is to be led by God and live the life that would make you say, "I want to be just like my daddy!" This book is dedicated to you!

LOVE YOU, DADDY!!

My son and I! (2012)

MEN! DO NOT SEND YOUR FAMILY TO CHURCH - **TAKE THEM!!**

Be Blessed!!!
Brother Prater

Contact Information

Brother Prater
(214) 908-3056
P.O. Box 224122
Dallas, Texas 75222-4122
Brother Prater (YouTube & Facebook)
Brotherprater@gmail.com (Email)